An Experimental Draft

(unfinished)

gayatri

Made with ❤ on the BookLeaf Publishing Platform

www.bookleafpub.in

www.bookleafpub.com

Dedication

for the six years old me, who wrote a poem about an elephant, thank you for writing!

Preface

There are days one decides on a whim, *and an experimental draft (unfinished)* results from one such decision. Poetry was something I never thought I would be writing other than scribbling bits here and there or on the backside of the question paper when bored during the exam. I seek poetry as a means to experiment and improve my craft and this collection is a reflection of that. Every day I wrote a poem as a form of exercise, and these barely edited poems taught me a lot about writing and gave me one of the most fun and fulfilling writing experiences.

Acknowledgements

My mother, my best friend, and my little cousin —the only ones who knew I was doing the #TheWriteAngle challenge, Thank you.

Thank you Krishnamayi for the cover for this book.

because kelly is a jellyfish

the little plastic doll submerged
water filled till the rim of the blue bucket
kelly couldn't breathe
kelly was a gift from my sister, the perfect gift
like the caramel sauce on the sundae from Martins'
Creamery
sweet and buttery with a tint of burnt sugar

barbie and kelly adorns the shelves of our house—
dusted and covered in cobwebs
placed in a corner—
next to a tattered English-Hindi dictionary (sister's
dictionary)

when it rained in October, the mouldy walls of the house
cracked
breaking the shelves in halves

cursed by a kraken or a sea monster—
our house flooded

barbie got lost
and kelly fell into the water

on the christmas eve
caramel sundae, brownie sundae, and banana split—
were brought from Martins' Creamery
sister took a bite of the banana split
and someone screamed from the kitchen
barbie was found—
half broken but undead

we ate our sundae in silence
Martins' Creamery became a forgotten memory

on the New Year's Eve
we ate Neapolitan pizza from an Italian joint
kelly sank deeper and deeper
but was not forgotten
she kept swimming like a jellyfish

on February 7th
sister brought strawberry cake for my birthday
no one touched the cake
everyone kept talking,
the birthday wishes were muffled
and everyone talked about kelly

in the fridge I placed the caramel sundae from Martins'
Creamery
no one noticed
everyone babbled on about kelly

kelly couldn't breathe sister said
kelly would die someone else said
kelly died, another said

but kelly kept swimming because kelly is a jellyfish

mango cheese cake

Sat on the porch with half peeled orange and a mango cheesecake
it tasted sweet and of your home
saved the last bit for the night to devour as a midnight snack
for your kiss lingered in every bite
I yearn to eat it over and over
till the taste gets tattooed in my mouth
and I get sick of it

summer of '19

you look like the summer of '19
sweet tea, bombay toast, and the unsolved calculus
equation
summer rains, holidays, and the heat wave
you are loved and loathed
like the memory of summer of '19

coffee toffee

Kishore Kumar hits from the 60s plays in the background and the room tastes of filter coffee

Amma returns from the temple with an unniappam

And I dash to the bathroom with unniappam in my mouth

half solved trigonometric equations and an untouched Hindi essay

I hurry to the bus stop

stuffed with students from different schools, the quiet morning is noisy

closed shops and endless chatter, waiting for bus is torture

A girl from another school offered a coffee flavoured toffee

"it helps," she said and smiled

Toffee tasted heavenly or maybe I am being a bit dramatic

Climbing on to the bus, I turned to her

She waved, and I waved back

But forgot to say, 'the toffee is the best thing that ever happened!'

5. ghost

ghost, my companion
the one who keeps me safe
when it rains outside
or when it snows in the anime
when I eat frozen four cheese pizza
or when Naruto eat tonkotsu miso ramen
there is a presence, hovering over
mouldy walls and cracked ceiling
water drips yet not a drop fall
covered by an invisible umbrella, the ghost protects
howling of neighbour's bloodhound and the pale face of
courier boy
everyone sees the ghost
 except me

fly me to Tokyo

fly me to Tokyo, let me count ichi ni san

do you think the water will taste sweeter or will it remind me of you?

will I find you in the streets of Tokyo, or will I have to travel farther away?

fly me to Kyoto, let me count shi go roku

can we spend the day tasting sake, touring breweries?

will the streets of Kyoto help me slip away from you or should I travel farther and farther away?

fly me back home, let me count nana hachi kyu

will the smell of udon from the local Japanese café takes me back to Tokyo?

let me count again ichi ni san

will you be there when I open my eyes? or will I be back in streets of Tokyo looking for you?

fanfic

mouldy rooms, closed doors, and the flickering light
from the Vivobook 15
turn the room to a cardboard box
but the fluorescent light from grand pa's torch lit the
faded blue walls
making the cardboard box feel like a makeshift room
white noise from the damaged speaker filled the air
but grand ma's prayers faint against the splattering
sound of rain, turned the room to somewhat like home
the buzzing of mosquito irritated me as I typed the last
chapter of an abandoned fanfic
the *itafushi* fanfic flashed on AO3
the rain softened and grandma's prayer got louder as I
scrolled through the comments
gojosnaccc spammed the comments
and it was probably the best encouragement
black tea on the table turned cold and my half-opened
Jujutsu Kaisen (vol 22) fell down
a strange dread and giddiness filled me as I posted new
chapter

the fluorescent light from grandpa's touch turned
brighter
and the little mouldy cardboard box felt more like home

maybe it is a red string of fate!

I find you in stillness
frozen yoghurt and burnt cake
evening torrents and the quiet thunder
you stay, unmoving
still as the pebble on grandpa's table

I find you in chaos
chocolate cake batter and whipped cream
crowded lanes of *Chandni Chowk* and in the ghee
dipped parathas from *Paranthe wali Gali*
you followed, like the moon
always moving as the train travelled through cities

You were everywhere
In the food I ate, in the places I visited
In the books I read, and in the songs, I heard
but it took me years to understand

to find you both in my everyday chaos and stillness

21 moons

so much sadness in you that when you died, the birds of
the Glass Town ruptured and all the twenty-one moons
vanished
Mama heard the crack and wept for days
and I sat on the sofa, dreaming of days we could have
lived
Mama called you a child with sorrowful eyes
and I fancied having your eyes, it would be like being the
saddest poem or it would be like being the moon
you loved the moons—all twenty-one of them, each one
for the year you lived
you counted them every night
I imagined being you
I imagine being loved
I imagined being pitied
and I imagined being sad
it was hard, but it felt natural to be you
for I loved you
I loved the way you let your hair fall on my face,
the smell of coconut and scented jasmine intoxicated me

I loved the way you dressed, like a girl from a period
drama, all poised and rich
I loved how you cried and laughed
I loved the way you left the grapes half eaten
I loved the songs you sang
I loved you so much, that when you died, I wished you
will haunt me in dreams
I longed to be loved that I killed you
I killed you, for I hated the coldness in me
I hated the way I never felt your sadness
I hated the way I never felt being loved
 I hated the way I never even felt the hate
and still I missed you.
I missed you like the moons around the earth, all twenty-
one of them,
the ones that bleed and the ones that break,
the one we see, the one we will never know
and the ones that vanished
I missed you more than the moons would miss the earth.
and still you never returned

stardust, moonlight

stardust, moonlight
looking at him feels like a fever dream
(is he the one Marlowe meant when he said, "Was this
the face that launched a thousand ships...")
green vest, with double lid- mono lid eyes
the world blurs and every spotlight on him
he is a spell that bewitches you
looking at him feels like a fever dream
stardust, moonlight

monsters

you called us the monsters burrowed in the sea
and like a white shadow lurked around, and casted light
into the depths,
you thought the light would devour us, but it was our
hunger that grew with time
we heard the song you sang, the one you stole from us
you called us the beast with maddened voice
that needs to be tamed and caressed
every day you come and dug your palms
deep into the sea in search for us
for the fool once said, the wicked monsters
dwells in the sea.
you come in troops muttering silly words
your half-said sentence beat along the wave
and we laugh,
an unsteady laughter that lulls your ear
and soothes you to sleep.
every night we see you— eyes closed, breath held, curled
up against another
cradled in the lost goodness,

we blow into your ear the song untouched by men,
you shiver and spin in circular mould.
slowly, slowly, you fall
deep into the abyss
and darkness prevail.

you

summer rain, blueberry ice candy, and the lime juice from uncle joy's bakery
ice candy melts and the sourness of the lime juice lingers as I wait for you
an hour, a minute, a second—rain comes and goes, but you never come

sticky hands, muddied slippers, and the rickshaw ride to metro station
broken umbrella and the horde of people suffocates as my thoughts stay with you
an hour, a minute, a second—train comes and goes, but I never get on one

rotten jasmine garland, dried rose, and a chocolate wrapper lie on the station bench
The Exorcist soundtrack and the WhatsApp notification pops as I was lost in the memories of you
an hour, a minute, a second—rain stops, train comes and I find myself going home

they say we cry an ocean

they say we cry an ocean
sea turtles, seaweeds, coral reefs
wreck gods and ruin temples

they say we cry an ocean
seabirds, seashells, cuttlefish bones
dismantle the system and disrupt peace

they say we cry an ocean
shipwrecks, plastic litter, cigarette butts
vanquished and hollow,

with nothing left but the ocean

twenty two

Do you ever live in a song?
Where you are forever twenty-two
And stuck in a loop?
bhalla papdi, aloo tikki, sev puri
still greased in the corners of your mouth
morning traffic, half opened shops, crowded buses
memory so vivid, it feels like yesterday
from *The Iliad, The Odyssey,* and *Paradise Lost*
to *Don Quixote* and *The Stranger,*
literature is all you eat and swallow
like a gastric patient on diet and pills
twenty-two was glorious and ugly
twenty-two had hope
and when you hardly smile, you yearn for that hope
the song plays—
five or six boys in their twenties sing
about lost childhood and the not so beautiful twenties
but you go back in time
for there was hope
and hope is all you need to smile

the girl in pink

march rains and mint coffee
it was supposed to be a date?
dressed in white with a broken phone case
I sat next to the window, it was bay window
outside people flocked waiting for the bus
red bus comes and goes, but the crowd seems to be still
rained slowed, and the coffee turned cold
people swarmed around like bees
Hozier's *Cherry Wine* plays in the empty café
it no longer feels like a date
the chaos from the bus stop seeps in
Rex Orange County's *Sunflower* plays
and a girl in pink walks in
strawberry scent and rose gold hair tied in high pony
she smiles,
like a sunlight on a rainy day

stay, leave.

stay,

the cold apple juice and hot coffee from the machine
were placed on the cement bench

red and rustic, the bench reeked of humans

their sorrow, their grief, their anger, their hope and their
hopelessness

too many stories weaved and erased

and when we sat there, another story got etched

empty paper cups crushed, and a woman with a baby sat
on the cement bench

our stories erased and alternate stories got weaved

leave.

lonely goldfish

every day I wake up wondering what if the fish wants to
drown?
do you ever dream of drowning?
I ask my aunt's Goldfish,
a single goldfish in a large heated aquarium with 75
gallons of water
the fish keeps swimming and swimming and swimming
and it swims like Sisyphus rolling the rock up the
mountain
when all you see is water
do you dream of drowning too?
or does the loneliness drown you?

the girl, the green coat, or the umbrella

stained white uniform, monsoon rain
stood in front of the school office
and felt like as if stuck as if on a rollercoaster

orange peels, chocolate wrappers, and a one-rupee coin
were found in the puddle
a boy about ten took the coin
and threw his half-chewed bubble gum

students and teachers walked out
each looked either curious or appalled by my presence
the rollercoaster seems to have broken
and I was stuck in the air
unable to jump and unable to sit

but you raced to me with a green coat and an umbrella—
but we were fighting an hour ago?
"Because of a boy," you said with a laughter
and pulled me to a hug

you drenched and let the umbrella shield me
your green coat swallowed me whole
and I never felt so safe in life than with you at that time

was it the coat, the umbrella or you?
I didn't know then but I know now

midas ?

Glitter, glam and you turn everything gold
Maybe you are Midas
But you reek of the divine

You had nankhatai and flat white from a local coffee
shop
And the place became the most crowded café in city

You picked a poetry chapbook
Only for the book to become a bestseller in two weeks

You boarded a bus from an almost forgotten town
Only for the place to become a tourist spot

People flock towards you
Or you drew people like the Pied Piper
You are their lucky charm

Your touches are gentle and with caution
I yearn for you to touch me

Turn me into gold like how Midas turned his daughter
And let me watch the world cherish me in all glitter and
glory

Maybe you are a sorcerer or a witch
But you reek of the divine

when the world is ending

a rose, a lily, a glass of iced latte, and a packet of
cigarette
the room smelled of you
sound of flute brimmed in the air
words lost and recovered scribbled in blue on the corners
of the yellow wall
outside monsters are eating people
and people are eating monsters
but your room is crammed with music
you sat on the floor with flute and the iced latte
and a half-burnt cigarette between your fingers
music is loud, louder than the cries of the monsters and
people
so loud that it almost makes one feel your music could
save the world
monsters keep eating people
and people keep eating monsters
the world is ending, it's just us and your music
could your music save the world?
or should we let the world crumble?

a farewell of sorts

stars fall like confetti, and the grief visits you every
Thursday
it is a holy day
where to mourn is considered sacred
and yet we don't mourn,
we celebrate but they say it's the end of the world
and it is the end of our world
as we are forced to leave the Neverland
the rottenness and the holiness
and grief will no longer be our constant
but a visitor who greets us on Thursday mornings!!!